To make something so early on in life that holds all of your dreams,
and takes you wherever you find yourselves going.

Thank you to anyone who has purchased this book, proceeds of which
will go towards keeping us rolling for another 5 years.

C & L

THE ROLLING HOME

80000 Miles and counting in a self build home.

Calum Creasey & Lauren Smith

CONTENTS

ISBN 978 0 9935356 0 4 | First published in the UK by Stokedeversince ltd, 2015. Second edition.

www.Stokedeversince.com | www.therollinghome.uk | @TheRollingHome

INTRODUCTION

The van started out like most, an empty shell, a blank canvas. It didn't come into our lives out of the blue. Instead, at the end of a long line of vans of all shapes and sizes that have filled my life from an early age. One of my fondest memories is being picked up early from school, whisked off in our family camper van for the summer holidays. These early years spent in camper vans brought so much happiness. We grew up landlocked in the middle of England, but often found ourselves with sandy feet and salty skin.

We bought the van in Summer 2010. It started life as a VW T4 panel van with 120000 miles on the clock. I believe it was first used by an engineering company before carrying motorbikes for the chap we bought it from. We tried not to rush into converting it, rather decided to let it transform as we discovered what we needed on the road.

This was my second van and things I had learnt from my first conversion really helped when thinking up The Rolling Home. We knew we didn't want to use modern materials, opting instead for timber. It may be slightly heavier but the slower you go, the more time there is to take in your surroundings.

The design is simple and moves away from the traditional design of side units and rock n roll bed. Living in a van for long periods at a time is made easier when everything has its place. Storage is key. The seating area and kitchen make for the perfect amount of space for the two of us.

Later came the porthole and hightop roof. These were very welcome additions. Both brought a few nail biting hours of measuring, re measuring and finally cutting with nervous hands.

The van has been the vessel to take us away from the mundane familiar roads of home. It shows the miles, the little spots of rust are reminders of adventures past. Parked atop cliffs, next to rolling oceans, Baltic pine forests and Mediterranean coves, it has taken us to virtually every corner of Europe.

We close the curtains, read by candlelight and could be anywhere in the World.

The two of us and our rolling home.

2010- onwards

We grew up in vans. I cannot thank my parents enough for sparking a passion that would go on to shape our lives.

Me and two of my sisters in front of our VW LT coachbuilt campervan. Circa 1999.

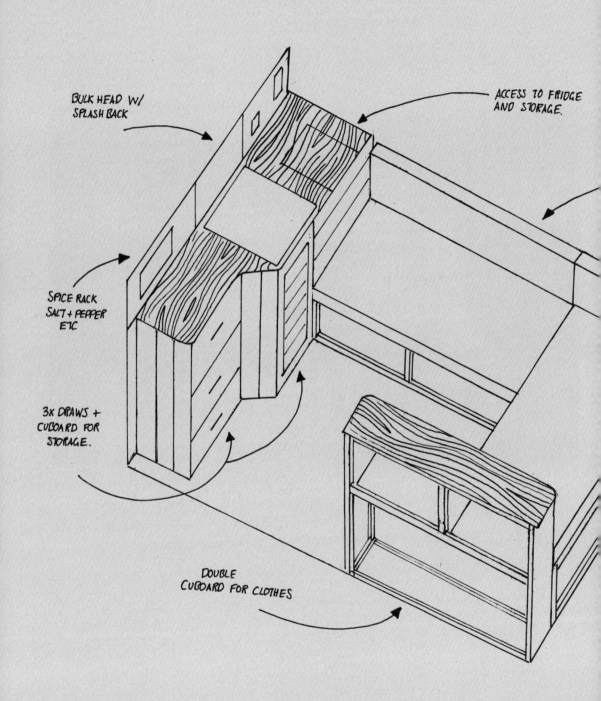

BULK HEAD W/
SPLASH BACK

ACCESS TO FRIDGE
AND STORAGE.

SPICE RACK
SALT + PEPPER
ETC

3x DRAWS +
CUBOARD FOR
STORAGE.

DOUBLE
CUBOARD FOR CLOTHES

A LABOUR OF LOVE

I think if we have learnt anything from spending time in a van it is this; comfort is the most important aspect of any small space. Being able to use the van for long periods, reading, sleeping, cooking and eating, it has to be versatile. Easily adaptable and hard wearing. Places for muddy boots in winter and towels to hang in summer.

The Rolling Home was a shell when we bought it. We opted to take a little time before starting to convert it. Laying down masking tape in all sorts of arrangements to find the best layout. The L shaped seating area that pulls out to make the bed is the best use of space that we could think of. We put in a bulkhead to separate the cab from the living space and this in turn makes the back of the kitchen unit. Our build is made solely of pine, it is lightweight, strong and cheap. Finished off with linseed oil, the timber takes on a really nice yellow colour. The worktop was saved from an old desktop and the stove/sink combo came from a boat.

The bed unit is made of sliding panels with bevelled edges. One thing to consider in a van is that the moisture content of the air can cause the timber to expand and contract. This means drawers and cupboards can bind or become loose depending on the seasons. The panels of the bed are bevelled to stop this and make the bed pull out smoothly.

Seeing any conversion come together is truly one of the most satisfying feelings in life. Building something that you will go on to use and cherish. Take your time and enjoy every second. *'Measure twice, cut once'*

FOAM BACK RESTS FOLD INTO PULL OUT BED

UNDERBED STORAGE SPACE

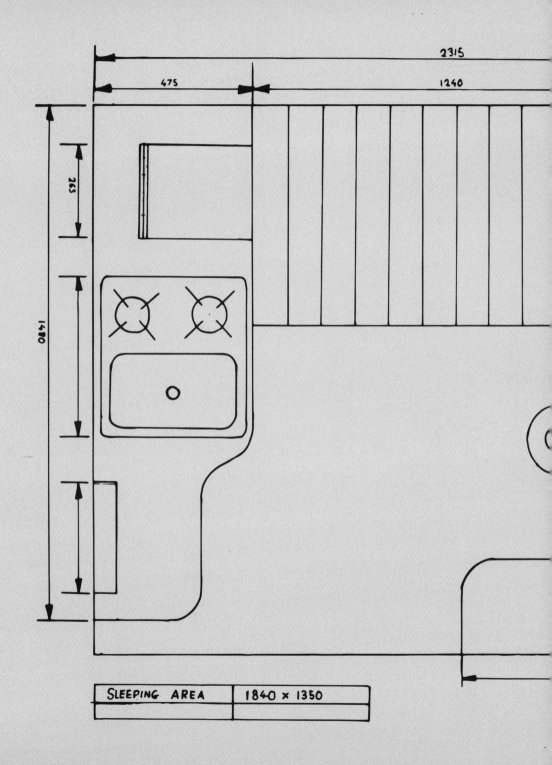

2315

475

1240

265

1840

SLEEPING AREA | 1840 x 1350

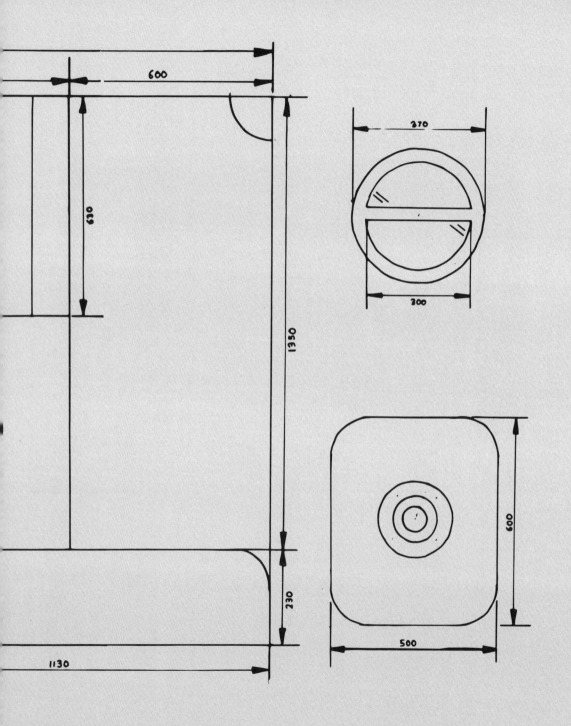

Shortly after cutting the roof for the hightop,
May 2013.

Pre side cabinet, *Autumn 2011.*

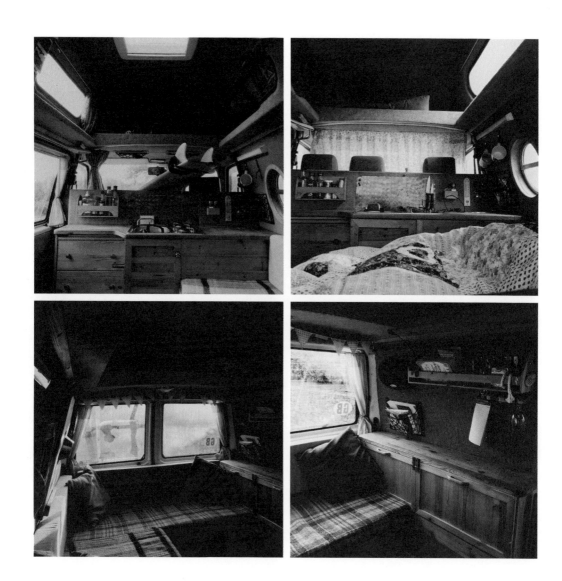

A view that never seems to get old.

The interior of The Rolling Home.

The day we removed the head from the engine.

Note the corroded 'water jacket' on the far piston. The cause of all our woes.

April 2013

Some days you decide not to leave the van entirely.

June 2015

A HEIGHTENED SENSE OF LIFE

When all things collide. After miles of driving, hot sticky cruising. We found our friends and were nothing but content.

Summer 2012 we headed out onto the roads of Europe once more. A little older but not much wiser. As always the day or so before our departure were ones of strange joy, slowly packing up the van for the weeks ahead. Making lists of tasks, checking the oil, topping up the radiator and tightening anything that may have vibrated loose. At this time Lauren worked in an office in our local town, a square room with square tables and filled with square dreams. She disliked that place for what it took from her, precious time. This is also before our first rented cottage together, not yet having flown the nest. We would pack the last few things behind my dads house. The same driveway we packed vans as kids. There are so many patches of oil and paint left there from vans long gone and I like to think The Rolling Home yearns for adventure just as much as we do. It doesn't look right sat in a suburban housing estate in the middle of England.

As always the boat is busy with pre school holiday families catching an early deal. Buses of school kids who have lost all sense of authority with the impending holidays and the first trips away from the confines of their parents. Having been joined by our friends and their van, we find a small corner and check the maps, not really needed as the road is one we have done many times. But I can't help but be filled with a little trepidation before any long journey in Europe. We opt for the later ferry to save our already small budget from taking a hit. The outcome being that we have to drive into the night through northern France, sticking to the back roads and avoiding the toll booths like the plague.

After what feels like an age driving, we spend the night in an Aire de Camping Car. The brilliant French have a much more open policy towards camper vans and put aside space for overnight stops. Admittedly not all are free and not all are very pleasant (think biffa bins, lorry drivers, general feeling of impending doom) but most are very appreciated.

The next day we wake to find that summer is in full swing and we just could not be happier. Filled with excitement we spend the remainder of the journey south with windows firmly down. The last challenge being the ring road that circles Bordeaux. I can feel its approach as Lauren is quick to remind me how much she despises this road. Smoothly through, and we can positively smell the Atlantic.

A day after arriving in South West France our friends arrive to the surprise of the group. Something planned by the boys. I do not know how but they managed to keep their trip secret and arrived in the dead of night after 14 hours of driving. We were delirious but overjoyed.

A good spot to watch the World go by, *France 2012.*

Jonny tying on bikes for the return to the UK, *France 2012.*

Making the most of having indoor
space wherever we please,
Summer 2012

A VW bay window squeezing between
the cork trees, *France 2012.*

Jonny making dinner at 'the spot',

France 2012.

The boys trying out their homemade
handplanes, *France 2012.*

Anna & Marie's beautiful Peugeot van,

France 2012.

Their window herb box was the envy
of the carpark, *France 2012.*

Lauren discovering the joys of
longboarding, *Summer 2012.*

Waking up overlooking Lake
Maggiore, *Northern Italy 2013.*

James finding joy in the flatness,
France 2012.

The week my Dad came to stay in The Rolling Home, *France 2012.*

Handplanes at dusk, *France 2012.*

The boys the morning after surprising
us with their arrival, *France 2012.*

Saving on washing up, *France 2012.*

Vieux Boucau after being woken at
2am by the French Police,
Summer 2011.

Wash day, *Portugal 2011.*

THE TIMES WE ESCAPE

I wrote these simple words on our return from our trip in 2011. We were fairly young and fairly naive, happiness came in torrents.

'I'm reluctant to attempt to document this trip in writing. I enjoy recounting most trips, however I don't feel I can do this trip justice in words. 3500 miles due south from the island we call home. Through France, North Spain & Portugal. Following the shoreline and meeting the Atlantic swell wherever possible.

I'll leave it at that.'

A perfect spot to cook dinner,
Peniche, Portugal 2011.

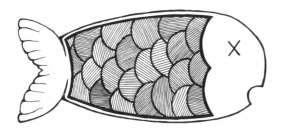

Sand dunes and deserted beaches,
Portugal 2011.

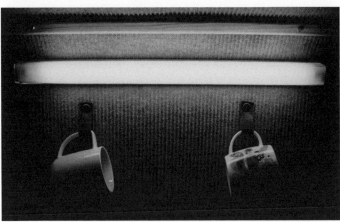

Last light, *Portugal 2011.*

Sometimes you find yourself in spots
dreams are made of - bikes, BBQs
and a beach that stretches on to the
horizon, *Pedrogao, Portugal 2011.*

Atop the Atlantic Ocean,
Portugal 2011.

The helm,
Spain 2011.

Plans scuppered in a supermarket car park, Southern France 2013.

ONWARDS

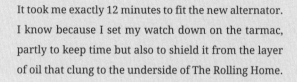

It took me exactly 12 minutes to fit the new alternator. I know because I set my watch down on the tarmac, partly to keep time but also to shield it from the layer of oil that clung to the underside of The Rolling Home.

Oh but If you could bottle the feeling, turning the key and hearing it fire back to life. Half way through. Half way through and we were tested, not massively, a simple part had failed, left us stranded. "Onwards?" I said. Turned to her and smiled. She has this way of turning to me at just the right moments. Spending that amount of time next to someone you know so well. You can feel the times they rest eyes on you.

Nearly 4 months earlier we had both cried tears of joy on the first drive out in The Rolling Home with its rebuilt engine. Genuine tears of joy. We felt free again, we were free again. The road opened up before us then, and here it was again. Here we were. Sitting staring at each other, I recall it being an age. I know thats wrong, it was mere seconds.

"Onwards" she replied.

Wild swimming. *Lake Maggiore, Italy 2013*

Morning light. *Northern Spain 2013*

Evening light. *Northern Spain 2013*

Underwater. *Unknown*

Billy & Jonny 'bronzing'.

Summer 2013.

Honouring the gods of the sea,

Summer 2013.

Galicia.

Summer 2013.

SHOWER STRUGGLES

Four days is about the time I start to panic about my lack of cleanliness. The dry shampoo is no longer working and the wet wipes are no longer sufficient for a 'wash'. What I need is a long hot shower! Unfortunately, unless staying on a campsite, this is a struggle to find.

Stocking up on water bottles for a road side hair wash is my preferred choice, although this can grab some unwanted attention. Beach showers; another good option, and much more accessible but again, turning up outside a beach bar with shampoo and razor in hand is not the best way to get on the right side of the locals.

Last resort has got to be gatecrashing said campsite. Hot showers, actual toilet cubicles and easy to blend in with the real guests. In, out, job done!

Shower struggles are not my favourite, but it's all part of the fun. L

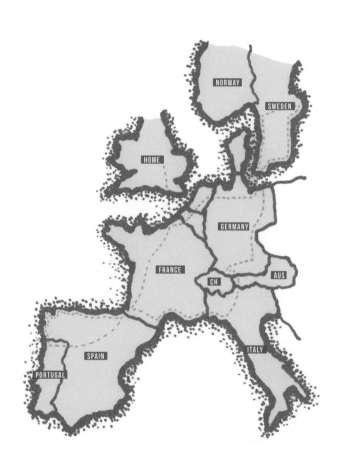

THE SMALLER BIRDS

We planned this for 6 years- do you have a definition of your life lived to the full? We now do.

I have struggled to describe it from the outset. I thought it was just buying a van and I was soon proved wrong. I thought it was growing up like I did, but I was proved wrong. We all thought it wouldn't, but life soon happened and we were proved wrong. We were destined to be different, to make our lives elsewhere. I met a girl in school and we were friends for a while. I never once thought I would spend the rest of my life with her, but I was proved wrong.

The smallest of meetings, the smallest of birds. The fleeting glances, those you don't think of, those you dismiss, can soon become the definition of your life. You will be proved wrong. She will be your life, and you will be hers. The van is a vehicle, the girl is a girl and your life is a life. But not just a life, the best life you can hope for.
Time to see it through her eyes.

Swedish landscapes. *Autumn 2013*

If those walls could talk,
Autumn 2013.

Teeth brushing,
Autumn 2013.

Every morning is a lie in.
Sweden 2013.

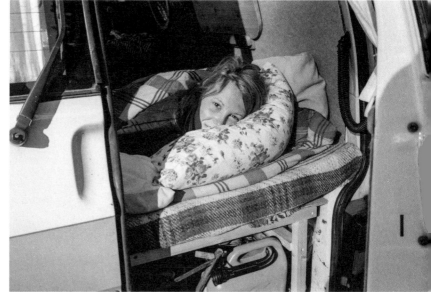

Scandinavian skies,
Sweden 2013.

Headed South for the Winter,
Sweden 2013.

Wild camp spots and beach
playgrounds, *Öland, Sweden 2013.*

Beach bags packed, *Unknown*

Stockholm Archipelago,
Sweden 2013.

Falling in love with the Baltic,
Sweden 2013.

FURTHER REACHES

NUMBER ONE

We have not truly travelled until we have sought out the

FURTHER REACHES

of the land on which we are from.

The Rolling Home lay in a sorry state, engine laid bare, daylight on pistons. Oil on hands and tarmac. Plans already made, those we could not go back on, with a lend and a borrow, we left.

Pete-

"Skye was a place where a lot of people used to go for the Cuillin ridge, the mountain ridge on the island. But also because of the remoteness of it. The water is clean, real clean. You can see 25 feet down. It is one of the best places in Europe to see sea otters. They built a bridge from the mainland in the 80s, they actually wanted to charge people to cross it. The locals didn't want a bridge, so the barricaded it.

There is no toll on it now, it's free for everybody - the way it should be."

14.2 miles

Go, travel many roads on many islands in a lifetime, yet the 14.2 miles that lay from Broadford to Elgol will be etched in your minds eye forever. The road gave a rest for weary heads, waking eyes and running falls. Forgotten gravestones are playgrounds for sheep. Moss breaks the bitten grass and clings to rocks amidst the sound of running water. Salt lochs eb and swell twice a day, jostling the moored boats that smell the Ocean, lying protected from its prowess. Freshwater slides silently across the surface of the dense saline expanse, hands painful from the plunge. The tarmac curves bringing back into sight of were you came, a moment of recollection for a first time wanderer.

As repe
fill the
guide,
thick ac
a quiet
we neve
the dau
our tiny
use of
smugne
have a

vn and diesel fumes
g fisherman, turned
ter isles through a
ed the crossing with
mes were given and
, for fear of tainting
pes that surrounded
ithtaking, a justified
Seals looked on in
knowledge that we
ney- they will stay.

As ropes were thrown and diesel fumes fill the air our young fisherman, turned guide, spoke of outer isles through a thick accent. We shared the crossing with a quiet group, no names were given and we never let ours slip, for fear of tainting the daunting landscapes that surrounded our tiny vessel. Breathtaking, a justified use of the word. Seals looked on in smugness, in the knowledge that we have a return journey- they will stay.

ALL ROADS TAKE THEIR TOLL

We would avoid toll roads. Instead choosing the slower, more picturesque back roads. The forgotten petrol stations, their pumps having run dry.

We have become used to emptying our bank accounts on numerous occasions to keep the van rolling. A new clutch just before a winter trip and pushing it through its MOT by the skin of our teeth. Our local garage has come to know the van well and in turn so have I. My fair share of oil soaked hands, scraped knees and an aching back. At the end of 2012 the van started to develop signs of a serious engine problem. Pipes bursting and losing coolant at an alarming rate. After trying every possibility we were left with the prognosis that the engine head was the culprit. Over pressurising the coolant system and drawing water into the pistons.

In December we took the van off of the road and sadly started to dismantle the engine. Three slow and cold months later, and with a lot of help from my Dad the van roared back into life. Those months of saving money and working on the van whenever we could solidified our love for it. We got to see it with all of the beautiful surroundings stripped away, its oily guts hanging out and spilling over the tarmac. There were times of desperation and frustration, but learning the inner workings of the van, the effect that numerous miles had on it over the years, felt like a right of passage. The notion that if we were to continue to see the World in it, we had to learn to look after it, to pay the toll all the roads had asked of it.

KIM & MAIE

Something we didn't expect to find at the end of that steep dusty track. We were searching for Campelo in Northern Spain, an idyllic bay penned in by sheer rock cliffs. The spot itself is hard enough to find, the locals having either robbed or graffiti'd the signs making it a tricky one to locate. We arrived late in the afternoon as most of the day trippers were clearing out, luckily finding a clear spot on top of the cliff overlooking the beach. The extremely steep track down to the spot isn't one I'd like to take again in a hurry. The slight smell of clutch and hot brakes giving us a warning. We were parked next to a German T4 and started up conversation with the guys when they returned to their van, we learned they had spent the day spearfishing due to the lack of waves. Kim and Maie rolled down the track about 15 minutes later in their T4, seems we had found a group with good taste. The guys were quick to come say hello and invite us to eat dinner with the four friends. A good few hours and bottles of red later, the fresh catch of the day consumed, we talked into the early hours.

The guys had invited us to stay with them in Ravensburg, South Germany. This fitted perfectly with our plans to make our way north to Sweden. Three weeks later we found ourselves seated around a small table enjoying lunch with the couple in their beautiful apartment they rented from a family friend. The two told us of their adventures in their own rolling home, of the winters spent in the mountains and their friends who all got together once a year to celebrate summer and companionship. We spent the night in the woods nearby, more of their friends arriving and surrounding the small bonfire. A circle of vans.

The time we spent with Kim and Maie opened our eyes to the beauty of new friendships, of taking time to listen to people and opening up your lives to others. We left promising that we would repay their kindness if they ever came to the UK.

FOOD, GLORIOUS FOOD

Someone wise once said, "When on the road, the only cares in the World are having enough fuel to keep moving, a safe place to sleep and enough food for the journey ahead."

Keeping the hunger at bay when travelling is something we always struggle with. Getting lost or a stretch of road taking longer than planned can make stopping for meals difficult. That being said, having a well stocked 'larder' is a must. Being stuck miles from the nearest supermarket is a real possibility. Tins of soup, dried pasta, rice and cereal are really great at getting us out of a sticky situation. The scaremongering aside, we absolutely love cooking in The Rolling Home, sliding door open in the height of summer or held up during a winter storm. There is nothing better for lifting spirits than cooking a delicious hearty meal on two burners. We have found ourselves cooking in some pretty amazing places, countless views that would trump any Michelin star restaurant.

We have two water tanks that hold 30 litres between them, a 10kg propane gas bottle, 12v coolbox and a twin burner stove. Plus a BBQ this is really our entire kitchen set up. The coolbox rarely gets turned on as it drains the batteries, although this does mean that we can only keep fresh fruit, meat and veg for a day or two. Rather than stocking up on these, it's great to hit the local market for ingredients for that nights meal. We enjoyed some of the best meat

ever in Portugal, found the freshest fruit and veg in Sweden and have had our fair share of baguettes in France. Salt, pepper, hot sauce, soy sauce, olive oil, balsamic vinegar and garlic, these come in real handy when cooking in a van and are a must. We have a small canvas bag hung on the back of our kitchen cupboard, a really great place to store onions and potatoes, away from sunlight, the canvas keeps them fresh and away from harm. Packet soups; not the most luxurious of meals, but these little wonders only need boiling water and take up no space at all. UHT milk- we have a bit of a love hate relationship with this stuff. Although, us Brits do love a good cup of tea and sometimes this is the only way of ensuring we can get our 'cuppa' fix.

We find food adds a bit of structure to your day. Either when driving, or parked for a few days by a beach. Breakfast, lunch and dinner are perfect times to chat about the next destination. Searching for groceries in strange towns is a great excuse to have an explore, to speak to the locals and try out our (poor) language skills.

Speaks for itself.
Galicia 2013.

Self appointed 'Head chef' Lauren
making Salsa Verde,
France 2015.

VAN FRIED RICE

Ingredients

- Rice (easy cook saves gas)
- 1x Garlic clove
- Olive Oil
- Vegetable stock cube
- 1x Leek
- 1x Red pepper
- Mushrooms
- 1x Courgette
- 2x Eggs

This isn't the prettiest of dishes but it is super quick and tasty. We always keep the essentials in the van, and chuck in our last few vegetables.

Start by chopping the garlic and add to a hot pan with a little olive oil. Add the dry rice (I know it sounds strange) and lightly fry for 30 seconds, this adds a really nice crunch. Add boiling water and the veg stock cube, leave to simmer.

Cut the veg and add to a seperate pan, fry off with olive oil and season well. Once the rice is cooked, combine with the veg. Keep on the heat and crack in the eggs, stir round until the eggs are cooked and serve.

For seasoning add soy sauce/hot sauce to your taste.

SALSA VERDE

Ingredients

- Handful of fresh Mint
- Handful of fresh Basil
- 2x Garlic cloves
- Olive oil
- Sea Salt

We love to make this neat little salsa with any BBQ. It's perfect as a side dish and packs a lot of flavour. Also great at masking any smoke/odours in the van.

Roughly chop the basil and mint and place into a small bowl. Chop (or crush) the garlic cloves, adding these to the herbs. Drizzle with a generous glug of olive oil and season with sea salt. Mix well and serve.

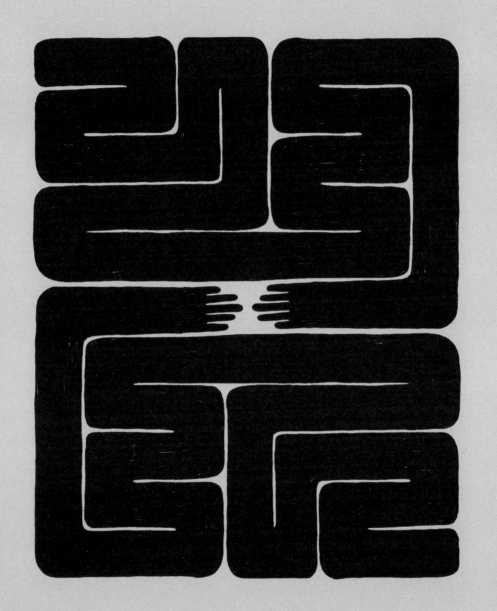

the intimate wanderers

the intimate wanderers - a celebration of the provocative nature of adventure. Companionships and human desires, mutual warmth on wanting nights and the sharing of the road. The overwhelming desires felt between those far from home. That glimmer of heat, the glimpses of skin. The smell of sun cream and of foreign perfume. An eclectic collection of memories of a life lived. The crossing of lines in the sand. The stories the grandchildren won't hear.

THE PROVOCATIVE NATURE OF ADVENTURE

THE STRANGENESS OF SMELL

Not eyes or ears that bring back memories more vivid than any, a scent of bygone times. For me this was growing up in campervans; a sweet, musty, earthy scent, of candle wax and surf wax, meals cooked, dry cloth, aged timber and diesel smoke. You can't buy or create that smell. It seems to happen by magic.

IN TUNE

Anyone who has owned and worked on an old vehicle will share this notion, and is sure to display a smile at the thought of it.

The tune we know so well, the click snap & rumble of a happy engine. If by some cruel act of fate the pitch or rhythm changes, the alarm bells start ringing. An unfamiliar, unwelcome tap, knock or bump. The unconscious thought that something isn't right. A loss of power and a sweaty brow. A warning light blinking on the dash. Hours upon hours of hearing the same tone from the engine, heart rate rising as the engine revs slow to a stop.

Life is about putting your feet up,

and keeping them up,

whenever you get the chance.

Boarding the ferry.

Dover, 2015.

No space up top for an old knee board,

UK, 2015.

Van rocket fuel.
France 2015.

'May all doors we walk through lead
to the sea'
France 2015.

Morning fishing in front of our camp spot

Guethary, France 2015.

Watching and wishing.

Guethary, France 2015.

Simple dinner, simple happiness.

Guethary, France 2015.

Speed blur.

Hossegor, France 2015.

'No overnight parking'
We have stayed in this spot a fair few
times over the years, arrive late and leave
early. The locals don't seem to mind
Guethary, France 2015.

Going nowhere fast. *France 2015.*

Max checking the bikes, *France 2015.*

We hope that the times documented in this book will inspire others to find their very own rolling home.

In our time of digital lives, make sure you know the smell of the sea, the feel of your lovers kiss and the ache of new adventures, all too well.

Forever onwards.

FOREWORD

My parents tried to teach me to value experiences over the ownership of material possessions. Instil in us the notion; it is not what you own, but the things you have seen, that make a life worth living.

The exception to this rule is The Rolling Home. This physical object has brought uncountable times of happiness to our lives.

Now the rust starts to take hold and the timber takes on a darker patinated character. The moisture and air claiming back the steel. The oil and dirt from many hands is left in the wood.

The concept for this book came to us a few years ago. It has been written, unbeknown to us, throughout the last 5 years. It is a compilation of times spent both on and off the road. C